FEARSOME, SCARY, and CREEPY ANIMALS

Killer Bees

Elaine Landau

Enslow Publishers, Inc.

40 Industrial Road   PO Box 38
Box 398   Aldershot
Berkeley Heights, NJ 07922 Hants GU12 6BP
USA   UK

http://www.enslow.com

14229280

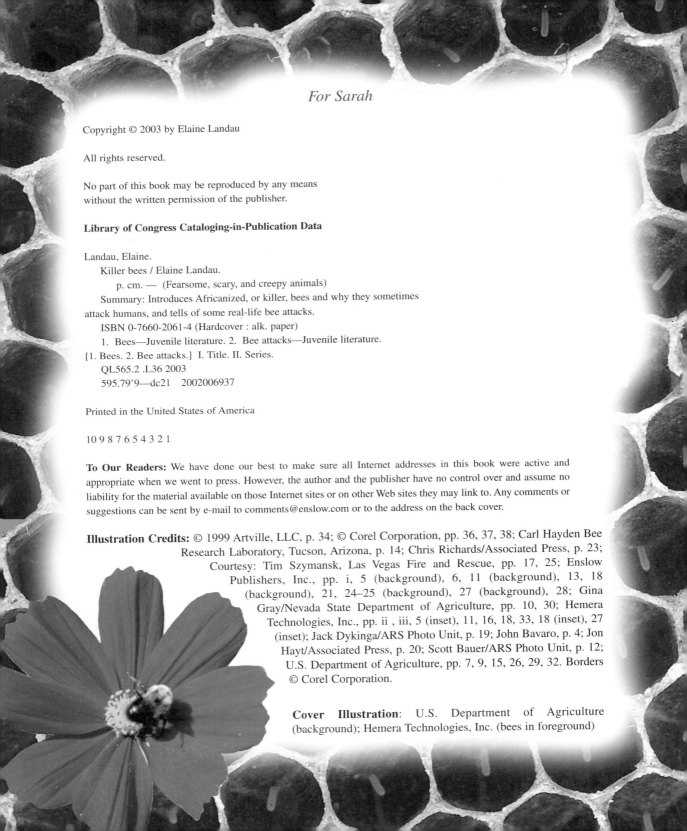

For Sarah

Library of Congress Cataloging-in-Publication Data

Landau, Elaine.
    Killer bees / Elaine Landau.
        p. cm. — (Fearsome, scary, and creepy animals)
    Summary: Introduces Africanized, or killer, bees and why they sometimes
attack humans, and tells of some real-life bee attacks.
    ISBN 0-7660-2061-4 (Hardcover : alk. paper)
    1. Bees—Juvenile literature. 2. Bee attacks—Juvenile literature.
[1. Bees. 2. Bee attacks.] I. Title. II. Series.
    QL565.2 .L36 2003
    595.79'9—dc21   2002006937

Printed in the United States of America

10 9 8 7 6 5 4 3 2 1

Illustration Credits: © 1999 Artville, LLC, p. 34; © Corel Corporation, pp. 36, 37, 38; Carl Hayden Bee
Research Laboratory, Tucson, Arizona, p. 14; Chris Richards/Associated Press, p. 23;
Courtesy: Tim Szymansk, Las Vegas Fire and Rescue, pp. 17, 25; Enslow
Publishers, Inc., pp. i, 5 (background), 6, 11 (background), 13, 18
(background), 21, 24–25 (background), 27 (background), 28; Gina
Gray/Nevada State Department of Agriculture, pp. 10, 30; Hemera
Technologies, Inc., pp. ii , iii, 5 (inset), 11, 16, 18, 33, 18 (inset), 27
(inset); Jack Dykinga/ARS Photo Unit, p. 19; John Bavaro, p. 4; Jon
Hayt/Associated Press, p. 20; Scott Bauer/ARS Photo Unit, p. 12;
U.S. Department of Agriculture, pp. 7, 9, 15, 26, 29, 32. Borders
© Corel Corporation.

Cover Illustration: U.S. Department of Agriculture
(background); Hemera Technologies, Inc. (bees in foreground)

Contents

1 Killer Bees 5

2 About Killer Bees 11

3 Attack! 18

4 "Bee" Aware 24

5 Bee Life 27

Fast Facts About Bees 40

Glossary 42

Further Reading 44

Internet Addresses 46

Index 47

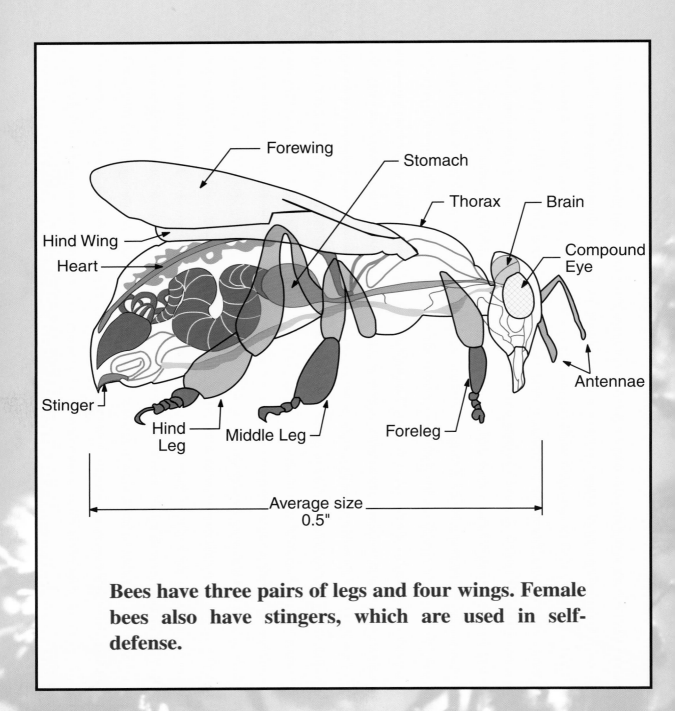

Bees have three pairs of legs and four wings. Female bees also have stingers, which are used in self-defense.

1. Killer Bees

It was a warm July day. Many people in Menifee, California were outdoors. Some were at Wheatfield Park. A junior league baseball team practiced there.

Eight-year-old Michael Carle was with a friend. The boys were playing in a field behind the park. They were looking for golf balls.

Michael found one. He reached down for the ball. That was when it started. A bee landed on his arm. It stung him. The young boy brushed the insect away. But then, something strange happened. A large group of bees suddenly surrounded the child. They began stinging him, as well.

Michael ran to the park. But the bees followed him. They kept stinging the boy.

The bees chased him for about a

hundred yards. In the park, the bees came across other people. They were stung, too. The insects attacked anyone in their way.

Michael Carle finally escaped them. But by then, dozens of bees had sunk tiny stingers into his skin. He had been stung about forty times. His face, arms, and neck were covered with bee stings. These quickly swelled. The stung areas were soon the size of silver dollars.

Bees are not usually dangerous to humans.

"I felt like I was going to die," Michael said later. "I was so scared. It felt like tiny needles all over my body."

Luckily, Michael received prompt medical care. He felt some discomfort, but he got better.

The scene left many questions. What really happened that day? No one would expect honeybees to attack that

European honeybees, like this one, are the ones we usually see in backyards, on flowers, and flying through the air.

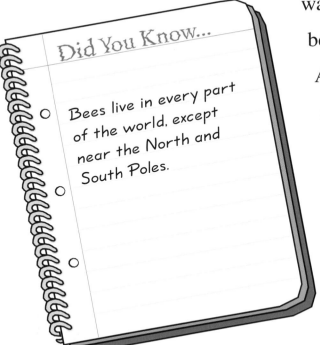

way. These were not average bees, however. They were Africanized bees—the bees also known as killer bees.

Africanized bees are related to African bees. African bees were once only found in southern Africa. But in 1956, they were brought to Brazil. Scientists there were working with bees. They hoped to develop a new type of honeybee.

Honeybees are common in the United States. The ones here are European honeybees. They have lived well with humans for hundreds of years. These bees are fairly gentle. They are also good honey producers.

But European honeybees do not do well in Brazil. The country's climate is too warm for them. They do not produce much honey there. Some die from the extreme heat. The Brazilian scientists wanted to change this. They needed a way to boost honey production.

The scientists thought about the African honeybee. It is fiercer than the European honeybee. But African bees are also hardier. They do well in hot weather.

The scientists decided to breed the African honeybee with the European one. This would create a hybrid—a new type of bee. It was thought that the new bee would have the best traits of both honeybees. It would be as hardy as the African bee, but as gentle as the European bee.

That never happened. The ideal tropical honeybee was never bred. Instead, there was an

Scientists decided to breed a new type of bee.

9

accident. A beekeeper let out the African bees. They escaped into the wild and quickly spread. They took over the European honeybee hives. As a result, a new hybrid was created after all. It was called the Africanized bee. But it was nothing at all like the hybrid the scientists wanted.

Africanized bees are very aggressive. They attack in large groups. These bees have been known to stay in these groups for days. They can chase a person or an animal for up to a quarter mile. In some cases, several thousand bees have been involved in an attack.

Africanized bees, like these, can chase people and animals in large groups.

These Africanized bees did not remain in Brazil. Since 1957, they have swept northward. Over the last forty years, they have killed more than 1,000 people—eight in the United States.

2. About Killer Bees

Africanized honeybees seem fierce. They do not look that way, though. They look like European honeybees. Africanized bees are a bit smaller. But the difference is very slight. It is not enough to tell the two apart. Even experts find it hard to tell. They have to measure twenty different parts of the bee's body. They also test the bee to be sure.

All honeybee bodies have three sections. These are the head, thorax or chest, and abdomen. These insects have six legs and two sets of wings. They also have slim pointed antennae, or feelers. The antennae have tiny sense organs. The sense organs help the bee to smell.

Honeybees have five eyes. Three of these are small. They form a triangle on top of the insect's head.

European bees, like this one, look the same as Africanized bees.

It is difficult to tell Africanized bees from other types of bees. These scientists are looking at the chemical makeup of Africanized bees, as compared to European bees.

The other two eyes are larger. The honeybee has one of these on each side of its head. Honeybees can see some colors. They can also see shapes. This helps them spot different flowers.

A honeybee's body is covered with small coarse hairs. Different honeybees may be black or brown. They have yellow stripes across their abdomens.

The honeybee's stinger connects to its abdomen. The stinger is straight and pointed. It has tiny hooks or barbs on it. The stinger is attached to special glands in the bee. These glands produce a poisonous substance known as venom.

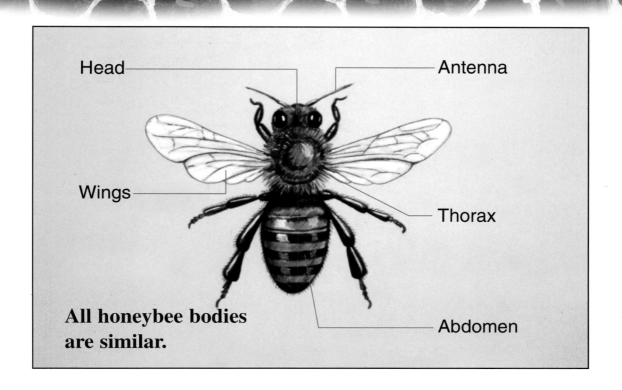

Head — — Antenna

Wings —

Thorax

All honeybee bodies are similar.

Abdomen

A honeybee's stinger is its weapon. The bee thrusts it into its victim's flesh. The barbs hold the stinger tightly in place. The stinger also has muscles within it. It works itself deeply into the wound. It pushes more poison into the victim.

After stinging, the honeybee flies off. The stinger stays in the victim. Leaving it there also injures the honeybee. It rips open the insect's abdomen. This causes

After a bee stings, the stinger and venom remain behind, as shown in this picture of a victim's arm.

the honeybee to die soon afterwards. That is why a honeybee can only sting once.

Have you ever been stung by a bee? It hurts. The poison worsens the pain. It causes swelling, too. Some people are extremely sensitive to the venom. They become quite ill from a single bee sting. If they do not get medical help, they can die.

Bee stings are not as serious for most people. But being attacked by Africanized honeybees can be dangerous for anyone. These bees present a different problem. They act as a sort of army. When one bee stings, it sets off an alarm. The alarm is actually an odor. It smells like ripe bananas. This alerts other bees to attack. At first, several hundred Africanized bees may sting. If the person does not get away, thousands of bees can attack.

Bees can see some colors and shapes. This helps them to find flowers.

Africanized bees are not comfortable around people and animals. A loud noise can cause them to attack. So can the scent of strong perfume. Shiny jewelry or dark clothing does the same.

There is little difference between being stung by an Africanized honeybee and a European honeybee. The danger is in the number of stings. When Africanized bees attack, the victim is stung many more times, so more poison enters the

An odor that smells like bananas tells the bees to attack.

victim. In some cases, people or animals have been killed because they could not escape quickly enough.

Africanized bees have been called "bees with a bad attitude." But this is not quite true. Africanized bees are not cruel or ruthless insects. They attack to defend their hives (homes). Their behavior is understandable. But in any case, you do not want to get close to their nests.

Never get too close
to a beehive.

3. Attack!

Killer bee attacks can be terrifying. People do not expect honeybees to be so aggressive. They are often shocked by what happens.

That is how it was for Charles "Steve" Handy of Phoenix, Arizona. Africanized bees attacked Mr. Handy early one Sunday morning. He was working in the yard at the time.

Handy had started up his lawn mower to cut the grass. A bee flew past his head. He tried to brush it away. "I swatted at him," Handy said. Seconds later, he was covered with bees. The bees stung Handy. They flew into his mouth. Some went down his throat.

Handy ran toward the house. His fourteen-year-old son was asleep there. Handy did not want to let the bees in. He thought they might attack the boy.

So, he tried to get a garden hose. Handy wanted to

Firefighters and other rescue workers use water and special chemicals to calm Africanized bees.

wash the bees off him. Luckily, his family heard what was going on outside. They called for help.

Minutes later, a firefighter rescue squad arrived. They got the bees out of Handy's throat. Then, they rushed him to the hospital. The doctors there were worried. Handy had been stung about 300 times. If the venom entered his bloodstream, he could stop breathing.

Bee removal specialists wear protective clothing to keep from being hurt by Africanized bees.

Fortunately, Steve Handy survived. His skin was swollen. He was also very weak. But his doctors described him as "extremely lucky." There were other bee-sting victims that morning. The bees flew over to a neighbor's yard. They attacked the neighbor and her dog. Happily, both survived.

The bees also attacked Handy's two dogs. The bigger of the two dogs lived. It had run away when the bees starting stinging. The smaller dog was named Armani.

He was a terrier-schnauzer mix. Armani did not run. He stayed to protect his owner. But it cost the little dog his life. As Handy's wife put it, "One dog was larger and knew to run away. Armani stuck next to Steve through the whole thing."

A bee removal service later found the hive. They think it contained about 50,000 Africanized bees. Armani never had a chance.

In other attacks, rescuers have been hurt. This occurred in Odessa, Texas. There, eighty-three-year-old Wilbur Roberts was attacked by Africanized bees. He was in his front yard when it happened.

Roberts' neighbor, Oscar Juarez, saw the

Some hives get so big they can house 50,000 bees.

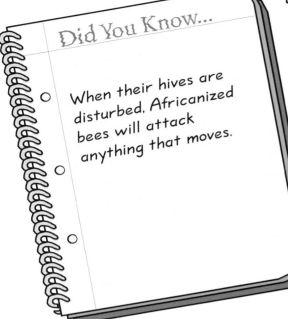

Did You Know...

When their hives are disturbed, Africanized bees will attack anything that moves.

attack. Juarez ran to help Roberts. He described what it was like. "He had hundreds of bees on him. He was covered with them. It was scary. I've never been in a situation like this. I was in Vietnam [the Vietnam War]. I would rather be shot at than chased by those bees."

Juarez called 911. Help came from the Odessa Fire Department. The bees attacked the firefighters, too. Four of the men were badly stung. One of them was stung twelve times. These firefighters were treated at the hospital. So was Wilbur Roberts. Roberts had been stung between forty and fifty times.

A second group of firefighters arrived later. They sprayed the beehive with soapy foam. It seemed to calm the bees down.

Scott Gardner is an Odessa Police Department animal control officer. He spoke about what happened that day. "It's common to get calls about beehives," Gardner said. "But it's uncommon to see an attack like this. These bees were unusually aggressive [fierce]." The bees had lived up to their nickname. They acted like killer bees.

Firefighters take the Africanized beehives away from places where people could be in danger.

4. "Bee" Aware

At times, even large pets and livestock have been attacked by killer bees. These include goats, cows, and horses. Three horses were attacked in Pahrump, Nevada. Africanized bees flew into their corral. They covered the horses like blankets.

Yvonne Smith is a horse trainer who was there during the attack. Smith tried to help the horses. But the insects also attacked her. One of the horses died. Its face was filled with bee stingers. The other two horses were badly hurt.

Usually, bees attack outdoors. But sometimes Africanized bees invade homes. This can happen when bees swarm. That is when they are on the move. They are looking for a new place to live.

In Phoenix, Arizona, 20,000 bees invaded a house.

They came down the chimney. Surprisingly, the owners and their pets were not harmed. Everyone got out safely.

The fire rescue squad came to help. Bee removal experts were there, too. The men put on padded suits and gloves to shield themselves from stings. Then, they entered the house. The bees completely covered the inside windows. Some rooms were filled with bees.

When Africanized bees are looking for new homes, they stay in swarms.

The men sprayed foam on the

25

bees. Next, they vacuumed up the insects. The workers filled four large garbage bags with dead bees. One bee removal worker described the scene as "pretty amazing." He had been in the business for thirty-seven years. But the business was changing. Bee removal services are busier now. Africanized bees have made their job harder. The work is more dangerous now, too.

Africanized bees can be captured using a special vacuum tool, like this one.

5. Bee Life

Honeybees are social insects. They stay in groups called colonies. Honeybee colonies live in hives. Bees often build their nests in trees, but Africanized honeybees will nest in many more places. Often these include piles of rocks, rotted logs, porches, sheds, attics, and garbage cans. Africanized bees sometimes even build nests in holes in the ground.

A beehive contains a honeycomb. This is a wax structure made by the bees. It has small compartments or spaces. Bees store food in these compartments. They also raise their young in them.

Different types of bees make up the colony. One bee is especially important. That is the queen bee. Bee colonies also have a large number of worker bees. These

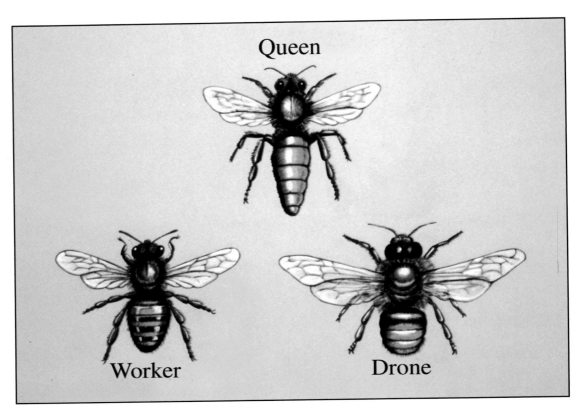

Queen

Worker　　　　　Drone

Bee colonies are made up of a queen bee, worker bees, and drones. are females. There are some male bees, too. Those are called drones.

Different bees do different jobs. Some of the worker bees guard the hive's entrance. These bees attack strangers or intruders. The threat can be a person or an animal. They alert other bees to attack.

The queen bee has a special job. She lays eggs. At

times, queens lay as many as 2,000 eggs a day. Drones mate with the queen bee. That is their only job. The drones deposit fertilizing fluid inside the queen's abdomen. The fluid remains there. The queen will release it onto some of the eggs. The eggs receiving the fluid develop into worker bees. Those that do not get it become drones. All honeybees reproduce this

Queen bees mate with drones to lay eggs. Shown here is a developing bee.

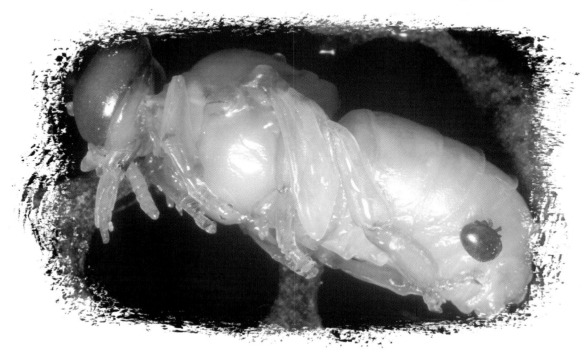

way. But Africanized honeybees reproduce more often than European ones.

Bee colonies can become overcrowded. When this happens, the queen and many of the workers leave. They fly off to find a new home. This is known as swarming. Not all the bees go, however. Some worker bees stay and a new queen takes over.

Africanized bees swarm more often than European honeybees. A large swarm of these insects may look

Sometimes, hives become crowded.

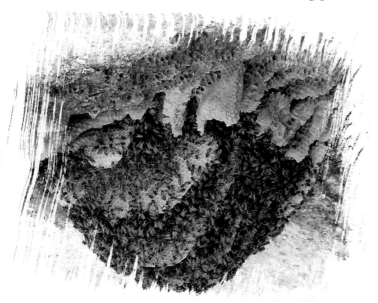

scary. But, Africanized bees become more aggressive once they have settled somewhere. Then, they are protecting their nest.

All honeybees get their food from flowers. They drink nectar from blossoms. Nectar is a sweet fluid. It gives bees energy. Bees also collect pollen. These are yellow grains from the flower. Pollen contains vitamins that bees need.

But bees do not just eat pollen. They also spread it from plant to plant. This pollinates, or fertilizes the plants. As a result, the plants reproduce. That makes honeybees important to farming. Many beekeepers have hives of European honeybees. They are used to pollinate important food crops.

Africanized bees can ruin this work. They fly in and they invade the European honeybee hives. Once they take over, the colony becomes more aggressive. The bees make less honey. They produce less beeswax, too.

Did You Know...

When looking for a new place to set up a colony, worker bees called "scouts" will do a special dance. This dance lets the others in the swarm know how far away the new place is.

Bees collect
pollen from
flowers.

Beeswax is another important honeybee product. It is used in candles, lipstick, crayons, and furniture polishes.

Over the years, Africanized bees have steadily moved north. From Brazil, they spread through South and Central America. They traveled at a rate of 200 miles per year.

By 1990, Africanized bees were in the United States. The first swarm was spotted in southern Texas. In 1993, Africanized bees were in Arizona and New Mexico. Attacks were reported in California and Nevada in 1994. These reports continued. In 2001, there were stories of killer bees in Florida and Georgia.

Africanized bees thrive in warm climates. But some people think that this could change. They fear

Candles and many other products are made from beeswax.

that these bees might adapt, or get used to colder weather. If this happened, Africanized bees might go even further north. However, many scientists disagree. They think that this is unlikely.

Africanized bees have been found mainly in California, Nevada, Arizona, New Mexico, and Texas.

In any case, the number of Africanized bees in the United States has increased. That has meant more attacks on humans. Today, people

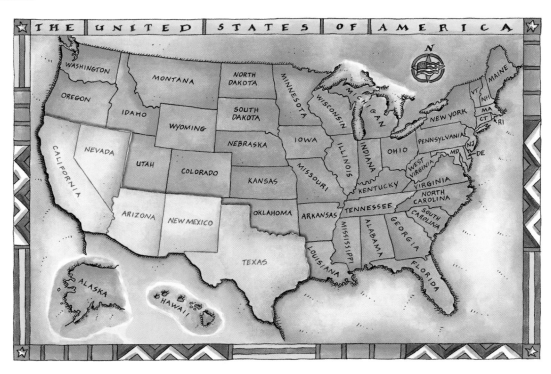

need to be aware of these bees. They should learn more about them. It is important to know how to protect yourself. These tips may be helpful in doing so:

❖ Stay away from any bee colonies near your home. Never try to remove them. That is a job for a bee removal service.

❖ Africanized bees sometimes build nests in holes in the ground. Be careful not to step on these.

❖ Learn which states have Africanized bee colonies. Watch out for swarming bees in farm or wilderness areas there. You should be cautious around these insects.

❖ In areas that have bee colonies, wear light clothing. Dark clothing can invite an attack. The bees may think you are a bear after their honey.

❖ Do not wear flowery perfume. You do not want to be mistaken for a plant!

❖ Be careful when horseback riding. Try to avoid low-hanging tree branches. There may be nests there.

❖ If you see a bee, do not panic. Most bees are just pollinating flowers. Leave them alone. They will usually leave you alone, too.

You will probably never face a group of killer bees. But sometimes, such attacks cannot be avoided. If it should ever happen to you, do the following:

❖ Run away as fast as you can. Be sure to run in a straight line. Bees are slow flyers. Most healthy humans can outrun them. Never try to stay and fight them off.

Be careful to avoid low-hanging branches when horseback riding.

Avoid running toward other people or they will be attacked, too.

When hiking, watch out for nests in the ground.

❖ Cover your face and head. Stinging bees go for these areas. If necessary, pull your shirt up over your head.

❖ Find shelter as quickly as possible. Go into a house, tent, or car. Be sure to roll up the car windows.

❖ Never hide under water. The bees do not leave. Africanized bees will swarm above the water. They will wait until you come up for air.

❖ Afterward, gently remove the stingers. Use a plastic card (like a credit card) to scrape them out. Do this as soon as possible. This reduces the poison entering your body. Never squeeze a stinger. It still has venom in it. More poison might be released into your body.

❖ Get medical help following the attack. Numerous bee stings can be serious.

Be sure to get medical attention if you are allergic to bee stings, or if you are stung more than once.

❖ If you see someone else being attacked, call 911 immediately.

The more you know, the safer you will be. With Africanized bees, it is best to "bee" aware and "bee" prepared!

Fast Facts About
BEES

❖ European honeybees produce five times more honey than Africanized honeybees.

❖ There can be as many as 80,000 Africanized honeybees in a colony.

❖ The Africanized honeybee will sting in three seconds. It takes a European honeybee as long as thirty seconds to sting.

❖ Some queen bees live for up to five years. During that time, they may lay nearly one million eggs. In the summer, most worker bees only live for three to six weeks. Drones live from five to ten weeks.

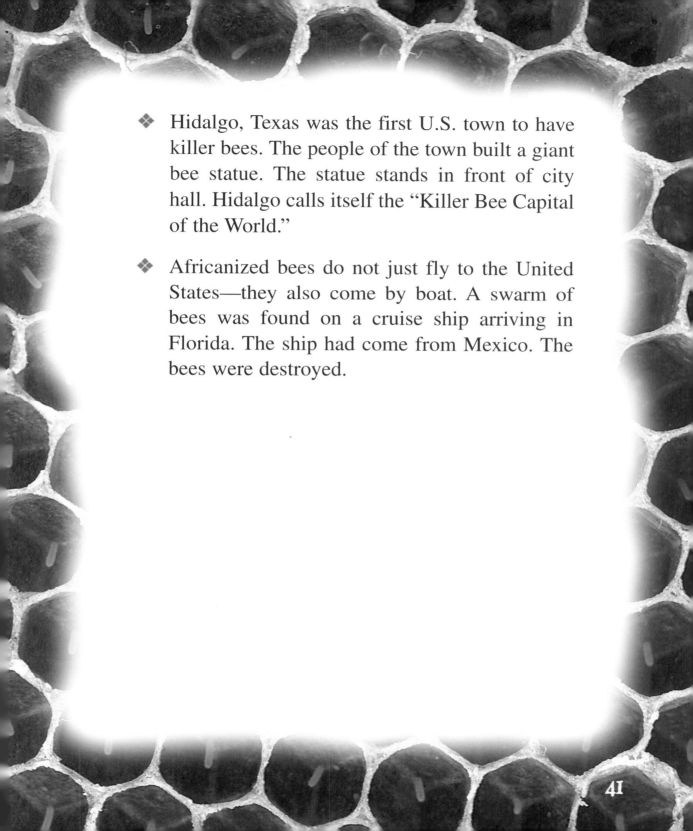

❖ Hidalgo, Texas was the first U.S. town to have killer bees. The people of the town built a giant bee statue. The statue stands in front of city hall. Hidalgo calls itself the "Killer Bee Capital of the World."

❖ Africanized bees do not just fly to the United States—they also come by boat. A swarm of bees was found on a cruise ship arriving in Florida. The ship had come from Mexico. The bees were destroyed.

Glossary

abdomen   The back section of an insect's body.

adapt   To change or get used to something.

beeswax   A substance produced by bees. It is used in making candles, lipstick, crayons, and other products.

breed   To mate; to produce young.

colony   A group of insects that live together.

drones   Male honeybees that mate with queen bees.

hardy   Strong.

hive   A natural structure in which honeybees live.

honeycomb   A wax structure made by bees.

nectar	A sweet fluid found in flowers.
nest	A place where wild bees live.
pollinate	The process of carrying pollen from one flower to another so plants can reproduce.
swarm	A large group of bees that are looking for a new home.
thrive	To do well.
tropical	A hot and rainy area.

Further Reading

Brimner, Larry Dane. *Bees*. Danbury, Conn.: Children's Press, 1999.

Davis, Kathleen and David Mayes. *Killer Bees*. New York: Dillon Press, 1993.

Hadden, Sue. *Insects*. New York: Thomson Learning, 1993.

Hines, Marcia. *Killer Bees*. Danbury, Conn.: Franklin Watts, 1998.

Holmes, Kevin J. *Bees*. Mankato, Minn.: Bridgestone Books, 1998.

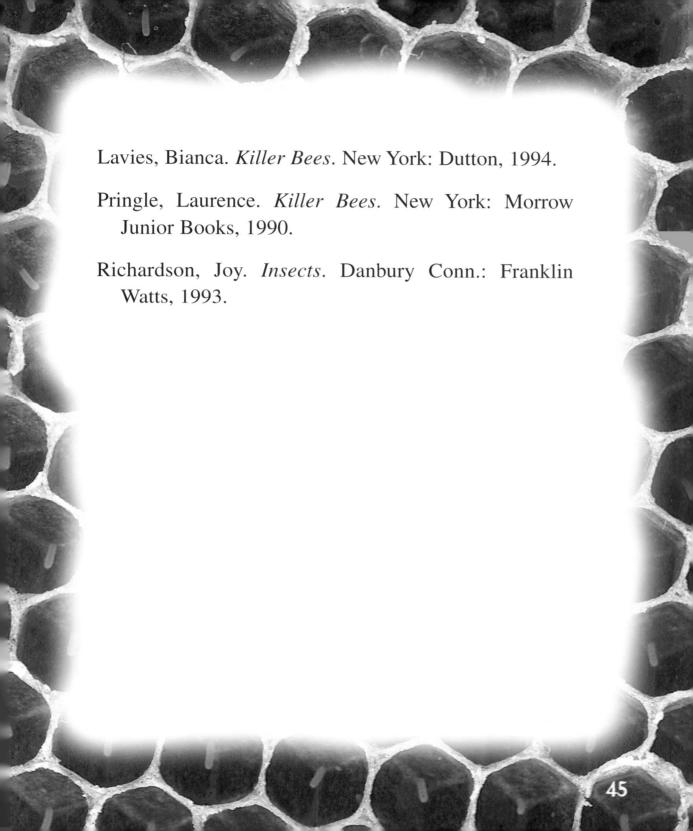

Lavies, Bianca. *Killer Bees*. New York: Dutton, 1994.

Pringle, Laurence. *Killer Bees*. New York: Morrow Junior Books, 1990.

Richardson, Joy. *Insects*. Danbury Conn.: Franklin Watts, 1993.

Internet Addresses

The Texas A&M University Agriculture Program

This site about Africanized bees contains information on safety, photos, and an interesting true or false quiz.

<http://agnews.tamu.edu/bees/navigation.htm>

The University of Montana

This site provides fascinating honeybee facts. Do not miss the special Kids' Section, which contains bee jokes, bee games, and bee trivia.

<http://biology.dbs.umt.edu/bees>

Index

A

abdomen, 11, 12, 13, 29
Africa, 8
African bee, 8, 9, 10
Africanized bee, 8, 10, 11, 14–16, 18–23, 24-26, 27, 30, 31, 33–5, 38, 39, 40, 41. *See also* killer bee.
antennae, 11
Arizona, 18-21, 24-26, 33
attack, 5–7, 10, 13, 14–16, 18-23, 24–26, 28, 33, 35, 36, 38, 39

B

beekeeper, 10, 31
beeswax, 33
Brazil, 8–9, 10, 33

C

California, 5–7, 33
Carle, Michael, 5–7
chest. *See* thorax.
colony, 27–28, 30, 31, 35, 40
cow, 24

D

dog, 20–21
drone, 28, 29, 30, 40

E

European bee, 8–9, 10, 11, 16, 27, 30, 31, 40. *See also* honeybee.

eye, 11–12

F

farming, 31
feelers. *See* antennae.
Florida, 33, 41

G

Gardner, Scott, 23
Georgia, 33
goat, 24

H

Handy, Charles "Steve," 18–21
head, 11
hive, 10, 16, 21, 23, 27, 28, 31
honey, 8–9, 31, 35, 40
honeybee, 7–8, 9, 10, 11–14, 18, 27, 30, 31, 33. *See also* European bee.
honeycomb, 27
horse, 24, 36
hybrid, 9, 10

J

Juarez, Oscar, 22

K

killer bee, 8, 18, 23, 24, 33, 36, 41. *See also* Africanized bee.

L

leg, 11

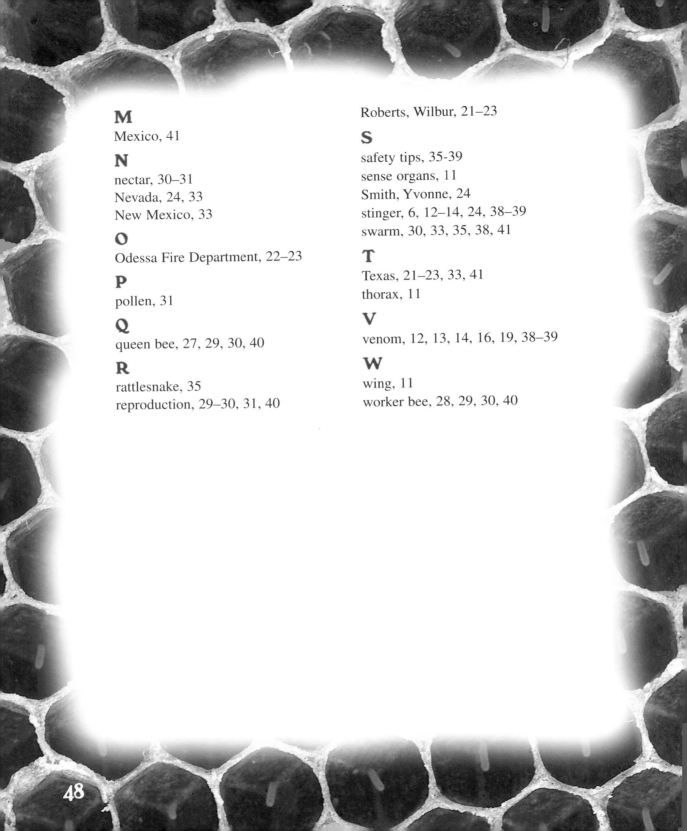

M

Mexico, 41

N

nectar, 30–31

Nevada, 24, 33

New Mexico, 33

O

Odessa Fire Department, 22–23

P

pollen, 31

Q

queen bee, 27, 29, 30, 40

R

rattlesnake, 35

reproduction, 29–30, 31, 40

Roberts, Wilbur, 21–23

S

safety tips, 35-39

sense organs, 11

Smith, Yvonne, 24

stinger, 6, 12–14, 24, 38–39

swarm, 30, 33, 35, 38, 41

T

Texas, 21–23, 33, 41

thorax, 11

V

venom, 12, 13, 14, 16, 19, 38–39

W

wing, 11

worker bee, 28, 29, 30, 40